ISBN-9780997855517

About this Book
"s"

This book targets the sounds "s" and "s" blends. One of the first steps to learning sounds or correcting speech errors is to increase a child's sound awareness. While reading this book, read slowly and take extra care to pronounce the "s" sounds within the story. Allowing your child opportunities to talk about the story and pictures, or even read part of the story, will help him or her practice imitating the target sound. Note that a child may become frustrated when asked to constantly repeat a sound he or she is struggling with. Instead, continue to provide clear examples of the target sound while you read and discuss the story.

This book does not replace traditional speech therapy. There may be multiple reasons behind a child's difficulty with speech sounds. If you have questions or concerns about your child's speech or language development, please consult your child's physician or speech-language pathologist.

Most important of all, have fun!

Talking Tales:
Sam's Sticky Sucker

Written and Illustrated by:
Erica Graham

Skyrai Publishing

Early in the morning, Sam decided to sneak downstairs. He was hoping his mom would still be asleep. You see, his sister had given him a small sucker last night. Sam's mother had told him that he could not eat it until tomorrow. Well, tomorrow is today and he could no longer wait to taste that sweet strawberry sucker.

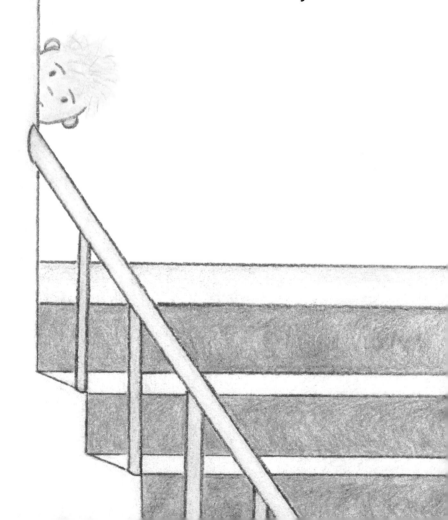

He snuck into the kitchen, pulled a stool over to the sink, and reached up to the window sill for his sucker.

He slowly removed the wrapper, being especially quiet,
and then swiftly stuck it between his lips.

Suddenly, Sam heard his mother's footsteps coming around the corner. Sam sped off to his bedroom, slid between his covers, and pretended to be asleep.

Soon, Sam's mother came in to wake him for breakfast. He walked down the steps and sat at the table. After finishing his cereal, Sam set down his spoon and was excused to go play. "Good, now I can eat my strawberry sucker," Sam thought. But where did he set that sticky strawberry sucker?

"I think I set it on the side of the steps," Sam thought. But when he saw the side of the steps, the sucker was nowhere in sight. "Now where could that sticky strawberry sucker have gone?"

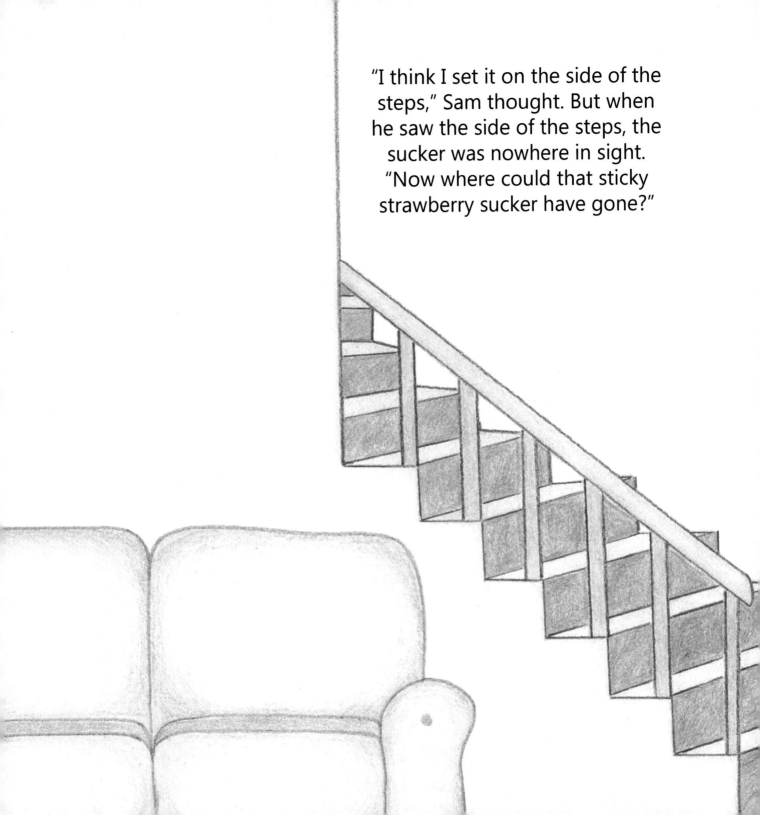

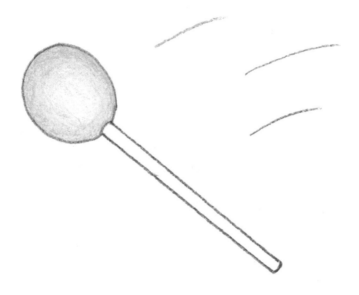

"What if someone slipped on it, sending it up into the air?
Then it may have soared onto the sofa," Sam said.

Sam looked on the sofa. Sam looked beside the sofa. Sam even looked under the cushions, but the sticky sucker was nowhere to be found. "Now where could that sticky strawberry sucker have gone?"

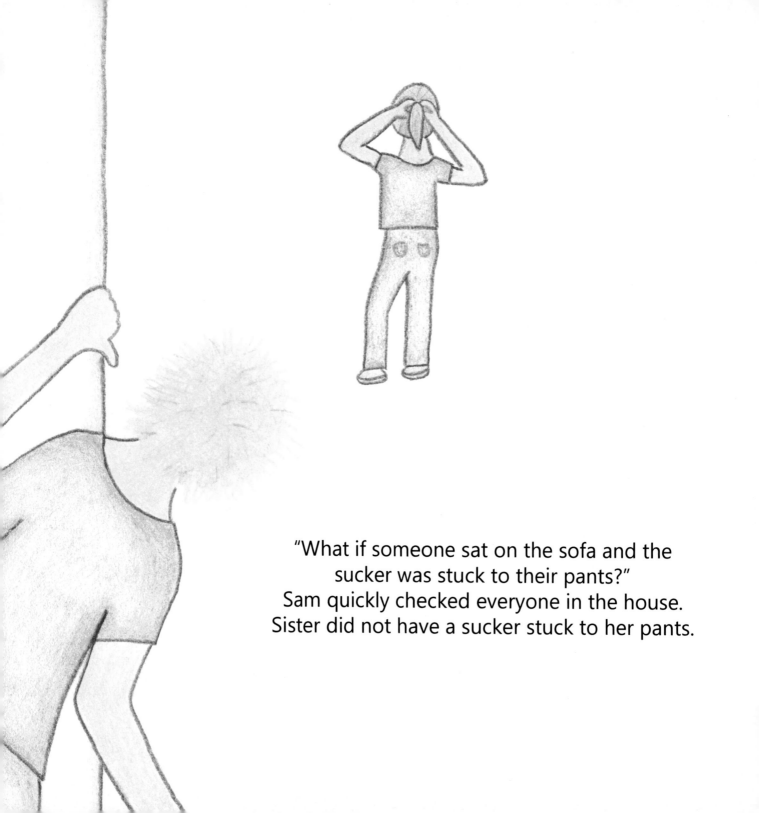

"What if someone sat on the sofa and the
sucker was stuck to their pants?"
Sam quickly checked everyone in the house.
Sister did not have a sucker stuck to her pants.

Mom did not have a sucker stuck to her pants. Dad did not have a sucker stuck to his pants. "Now where could that sticky strawberry sucker have gone?"

"What if someone sat on the sucker and it stuck to their pants? What if they threw their pants into the laundry basket?" Sam checked all the laundry baskets.

The sucker was not in sister's basket.

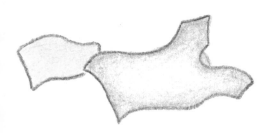

The sucker was not in mom or dad's basket. "Now where could that sticky strawberry sucker have gone?"

"What if whiskers the cat slept in one of the baskets, and the sucker was stuck to his fur?"
Sam scurried all over the house looking for whiskers.

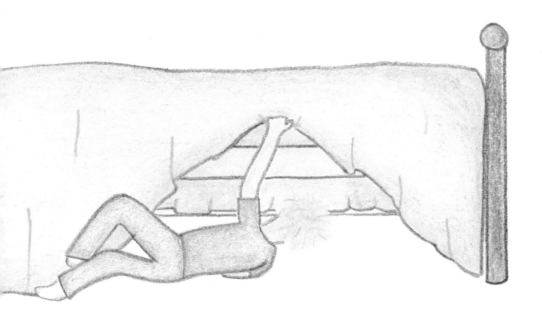

He finally found that sneaky cat sleeping inside the
bathroom sink. But the sucker was nowhere in sight. "Now
where could that sticky strawberry sucker have gone?"

Sam was tired after searching so hard for his sucker. He walked into the kitchen and sunk into the chair at the table.

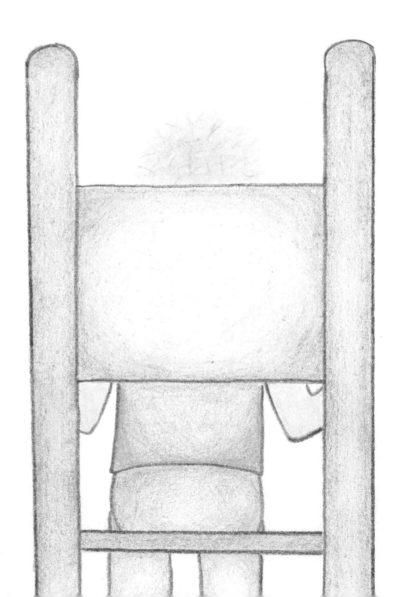

"*SAM!*" his mother shouted. "I am always telling you not to eat candy before breakfast. That includes strawberry suckers." Sam was shocked. How did his mom know he had tried to eat his sucker before breakfast?

"I didn't eat the strawberry sucker," Sam said as he started to sweat.

"Well, the sucker was on the window sill last night and now it is missing," his mom stated. Smiling, Sam's mom walked over to Sam, reached toward him, and smoothly pulled the sticky sucker from his hair.

"Now where could that sticky strawberry sucker have gone?"

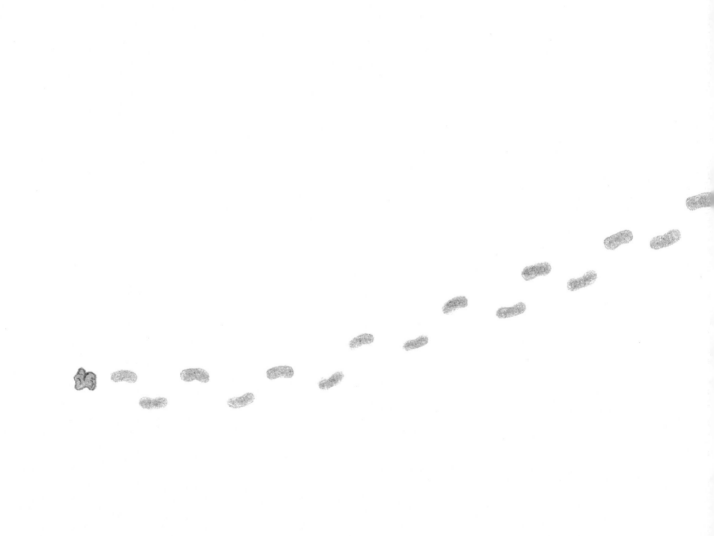

About the Author

Erica Graham graduated from Southern Illinois University Edwardsville with her Master of Science Degree in Speech-Language Pathology. She also holds her Certificate of Clinical Competence with the American Speech-Language Hearing Association. As a mother, Erica understands the difficulty parents have finding time to work on speech with their children. In her pursuit to create a fun and easy way for therapists, children, and their parents to enhance speech development while promoting literacy, she has written a series of exciting children's books. Each book focuses on a core sound used in the English language.

Outside of writing and working as a speech-language pathologist, Erica enjoys spending time outdoors with her husband and daughters, volunteering with the youth group at church, and drinking a good cup of tea.

Made in the USA
Middletown, DE
06 November 2016